How To Make A Christmas Tumbling Blocks Table Runner Quilt:
A Frugal Crafting DIY Book

Andrea Reynolds

How to Make A Christmas Tumbling Blocks Table Runner: A Frugal Crafting DIY Book Text and Photography Copyright © 2020 by Andrea Reynolds

All rights reserved. By payment of the required fees, you have been granted the non-exclusive, non-transferable right to access and read the text of this e-book on screen. No part of this book may be reproduced, transmitted, downloaded, decompiled, reverse engineered, or stored in or introduced into any information storage and retrieval system, in any form or by any means, whether electronic or mechanical, not known or hereinafter invented, without the express written permission of SkyShan Publishing, LLC.

LIMITED WARRANTY: Limited warranty on this electronic product. Skyshan Publishing warrants the electronic product will be delivered free from defects in materials and workmanship under normal use for a period of Ninety days from the date of original purchase. Skyshan Publishing will not replace the electronic product due to any loss this is considered out of the control of Skyshan Publishing. Great care was taken to ensure this product is accurate and presented in good faith. However, no warranty is provided nor are results guaranteed. Having no control over the choices of materials or procedures used, neither the author nor Skyshan Publishing shall have any liability to any loss or damage caused directly or indirectly by the information contained in this book.

For information regarding permission, write to: Skyshan Publishing, LLC. Att: Permissions Department, PO Box 13, Waldwick, NJ 07463

All rights reserved. Published by Skyshan Publishing, LLC
ISBN: 978-1-970106-38-1

A Note Regarding Copyright Infringement:

Thank you for giving this book a chance. Please be aware that most images in this book will have the above logo. This is to prevent the wholesale theft of my original work by others. Piracy is a real issue. While I spend weeks or months on creating original content, Pirates can publish multiple books a day by copying and pasting. The creation of this book took considerable time, effort and cost.

If you spot these photos in another book, please don't support thieves. Instead use your reviewing ability to inform others. Every little bit helps.

☐

Introduction

I have a confession to make. Most of my life is spent in a disorganized mess. My desk is covered in papers, and I am a neat freak's worst nightmare. However, when I feel myself coming down with the blues, I force myself to follow a plan. I transform into a compulsive planner.

I find that planning, organizing, and creating something from scratch helps balance my emotions. I chose this design for Christmas as I need to create a beautiful piece for a holiday filled with joy. Sometimes, I get bogged down in the commercialism of Christmas, and I need to remind myself about why this holiday is better with a personal touch.

By combining technology and classic quilting techniques, this project will take minimal time, and give you something tangible at the end. If you've never created a quilt before, this is the perfect project to get started on.

If you are a well-trained quilter, I apologize in advance if I do not use the proper terminology. I am a self-taught quilter, and have only learned terminology through osmosis. If you are new to quilting I have tried to define any terminology within the book.

I am also a little bit of an odd duck, so if you are a judgmental human, this might not be the book for you. I think I'm funny, but other people do look at me as if I have a screw loose. Sorry I haven't yet found a screwdriver that fits my personal screw.

In the following chapters, I will provide step-by-step instructions with pictures to create this beautiful Christmas Table Runner. I hope you enjoy the experience.

Let's get quilting!

Required Materials / Optional Materials (Marked as **)

FABRIC

For the Tumbling Blocks Interior
½ Yard (½ Meter) of White Fabric (With White Christmas Themed Fabric for accent)
½ Yard (½ Meter) of Green Christmas Themed Fabric
½ Yard (½ Meter) of Red Christmas Themed Fabric

For the Border of the Quilt Top
¼ Yard (1/4 Meter) of Solid Green Fabric
¼ Yard (1/4 Meter) of Solid Red Fabric

Batting/Bottom of the Quilt
¾ Yard (3/4 Meter) of Batting (Cotton/Polyester/Felt)

¾ Yard (3/4 Meter) of Christmas Fabric

Tools Tertiary Equipment
Sewing Machine
    **Walking Foot Attachment
    Thread – White, Red and/or Green
Pins – Straight and/or Safety
Scissors
Rotary Cutter and Self-Healing Cutting Mat
Iron
Computer, Printer, 2 sheets of copy paper, Glue, and an old folder

Creating An Informal Plan

For some reason, I love using graph paper to plan out a project. I could have just as easily used lined or copy paper, but I think I feel more formal. I'm not sure if this came from a childhood deprived of graph paper, but I love the stuff.

I create the plan, and estimate everything I need. I added the original plan I made for this project. This took about ten minutes, and I did make adjustments as I got closer to the actual creation of the quilt.

I started by planning the size I wanted the final quilt. Next I estimated the yardage I need for each color of Christmas fabric. I will always overestimate my yardage, because whenever I have followed other projects, I always use more fabric. I can't help it. I will make a cutting mistake at some point.

I determined that the size of my blocks should be 3 ½ inches (about 9cm) to give myself a 1/4 inch (0.5cm) seam allowance. I sketched the blocks roughly. Once I had the size of my blocks, I decided that I would make six rows of blocks down with eleven blocks across to fit the size I wanted.

3D Tumbling Blocks Christmas Table Runner

Shoot for Size 36"L × 15"W

Fabric (over estimate to ensure enough)

White = 1 yd
Red = 3/4 yd
Green = 3/4 yd
Back = 1 yd
Batting = 1 yd

11 squares total × 6 across

① Row A ▽ 2 △ 1 ▽ 2 △ 1 ▽ 2
② Row B △ 1 ▽ 2 △ 1 ▽ 2 △ 1
③ Row A ▽ 2 △ 1 ▽ 2 △ 1 ▽ 2
④ Row B △ 1 ▽ 2 △ 1 ▽ 2 △ 1
⑤ Row A ▽ 2 △ 1 ▽ 2 △ 1 ▽ 2
⑥ Row B △ 1 ▽ 2 △ 1 ▽ 2 △ 1

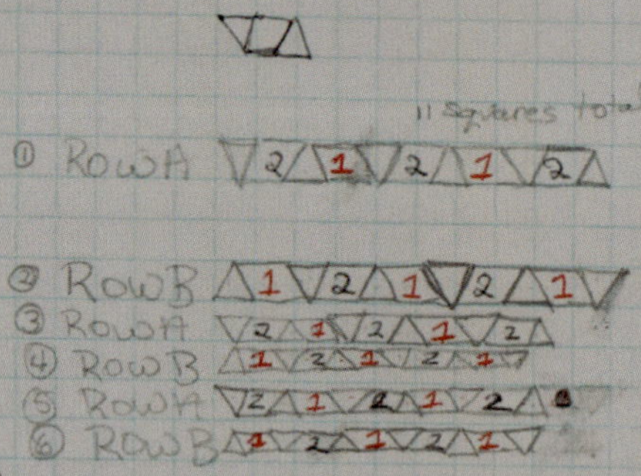

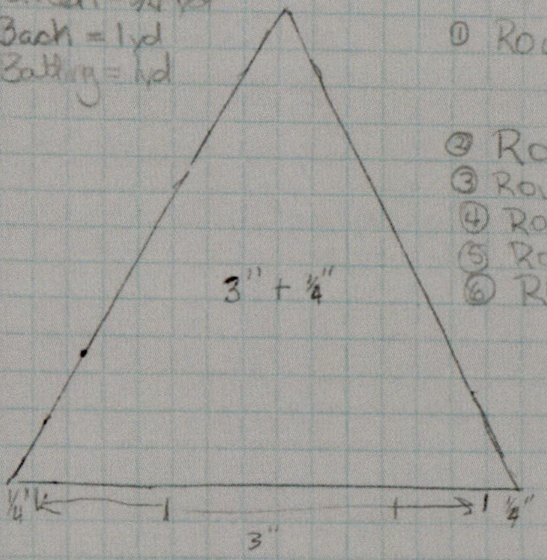

Triangle = White
Block 1 = Red
Block 2 = Green

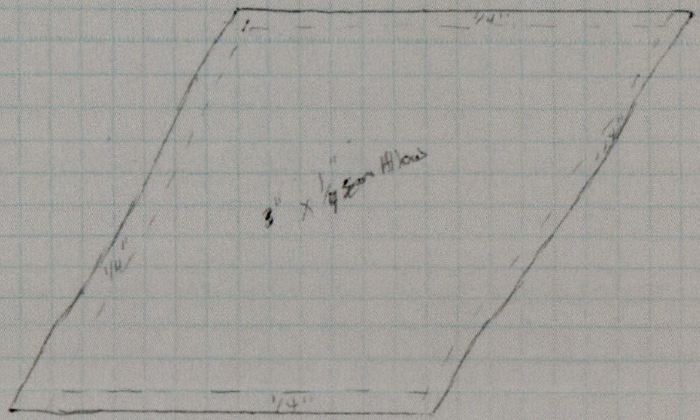

Triangle: 3" + 3/4", base 3", with 1/4" and 1/4" seam allowances

Parallelogram: 3" × 1/2" seam allow, 1/4" seams

After searching through my fabric stash, I found all the fabric that suited my Christmas theme. I also found a small amount of vintage fabric that I decided would make a great accent to the white fabric.

I have a very strong suggestion. If you have fabric that you think is ugly as sin, this just might be the time to utilize it. I love ugly fabric; tacky looking fabrics have made so many of my projects pop. The green fabric is so large and loud, but when paired with the red they complement each other. Put the fabrics together, and you might be surprised with how striking the combination becomes.

As I was exploring my fabric stash, I discovered a beautiful plain red fabric, and the opposite side of a green plaid was a fabulous Christmassy green. This is when I decided to use these fabrics to make an elegant frame, and prevent the table runner from being too busy.

Preparing Your Fabric

Now that you know which fabrics you *want* to use, now is the time to make sure that these are fabrics that you *can* use. I generally use 100% cotton fabrics, but every now and then I fall victim to the siren's call of a different fabric blend.

Choosing a satin or velvet sounds luxurious, but this is a table runner that will need to be washed if you plan on using it more than once. Every family has an Uncle Fred or Aunt Betty who spills their red wine all over the table, or dumps a scoop of mashed potatoes while they gesture wildly. I highly recommend prewashing your fabric selections. I use hot water, but any temperature is fine.

I do not put the fabric in the dryer, but press the damp washed fabric with an iron. I have had too many issues with fraying ends and wrinkles that won't come out without a ton of starch to trust these fabrics to my dryer. If there is going to be shrinkage, using an iron will give fair warning.

Creating A Formal Design

After verifying that I had the proper fabric, I created a more formal template in a spreadsheet program. I used Excel, but Google has a similar spreadsheet template. The proceeding page is the design I used while making this quilt. If you chose to make this quilt, I highly recommend bookmarking the template page.

I have a pet peeve with other tumbling block quilts I have seen. I really do not like when the light triangles are not the same fabric when forming the diamonds. I know some people make this design choice deliberately, but for me it drives me crazy. (Or I go crazier than the normal amount of insanity I usually possess.)

This quilt can also become a problem if you start piecing your triangles in the wrong direction. I prefer to prevent an error before it happens. In my experience, if I know exactly how to piece I can work quicker. In my spreadsheet I used the letters "V" and "n" to designate which direction the triangle should face.

Additionally, by creating this spreadsheet, I determined where I wanted my white holly berry fabric to fall in the design, and how many pieces of each fabric I would need to cut.

Christmas Tumbling Block Table Runner Design

	Block# 1	Block# 2	Block# 3	Block# 4	Block# 5	Block# 6	Block# 7	Block# 8	Block# 9	Block# 10	Block# 11
Row # 1	A V	2	A n	1	A V	2	A n	1	A V	2	A n
Row # 2	A2 n	1	A V	2	A n	1	A V	2	A2 n	1	A V
Row # 3	A2 V	2	A2	1	A2 n	2	A2 n	1	A2 V	2	A2 n
Row # 4	A n	1	A2 V	2	A2 V	1	A2 V	2	A n	1	A2 V
Row # 5	A V	2	A n	1	A V	2	A n	1	A V	2	A n
Row # 6	A n	1	A V	2	A n	1	A V	2	A n	1	A V

Key=
- 1 = Red
- 2 = Green
- A = White Triangle
- A2 = Holly Berries

□ or= □ *These are matching squares that form a diamond*
Make sure to use the same fabric to form the diamond

V = Triangle Facing Up
n = Triangle Pointing Down

Total Blocks=
- 1 = 15
- 2 = 15
- A = 24
- A2 = 12

CREATING FABRIC CUTTING TEMPLATES USING THE COMPUTER

I admit to a touch of frugality. I cannot justify spending good money on something I may only use once, when I can easily make the same thing for dare I say…CHEAP.

If you own acrylic quilting templates, I'm happy for you. However, I tend to make my own. I do have a ruler and self-healing cutting mat, which I utilize with the templates I make.

The one thing that always surprises me is the amount of geometry in quilting. This table runner quilt uses a triangle and a parallelogram shape to create a mesmerizing 3D effect. Without an acrylic template, you might be worried that you cannot produce the shapes needed, but if you have a computer and a printer you are all set.

With technology, you can make shapes easily in multiple computer programs. In the following pages, I will show you how to make these templates in Word, which can easily be made in other programs as well. I have embedded screen shots so you can see what I am referring to. I prefer showing rather than telling when it comes to computer instructions.

Open up Word, and have a blank document. Change the orientation of the paper from Portrait to Landscape. Then click on the "Insert" tab and then the box "Shapes." Choose the "Isosceles Triangle" option under basic shapes.

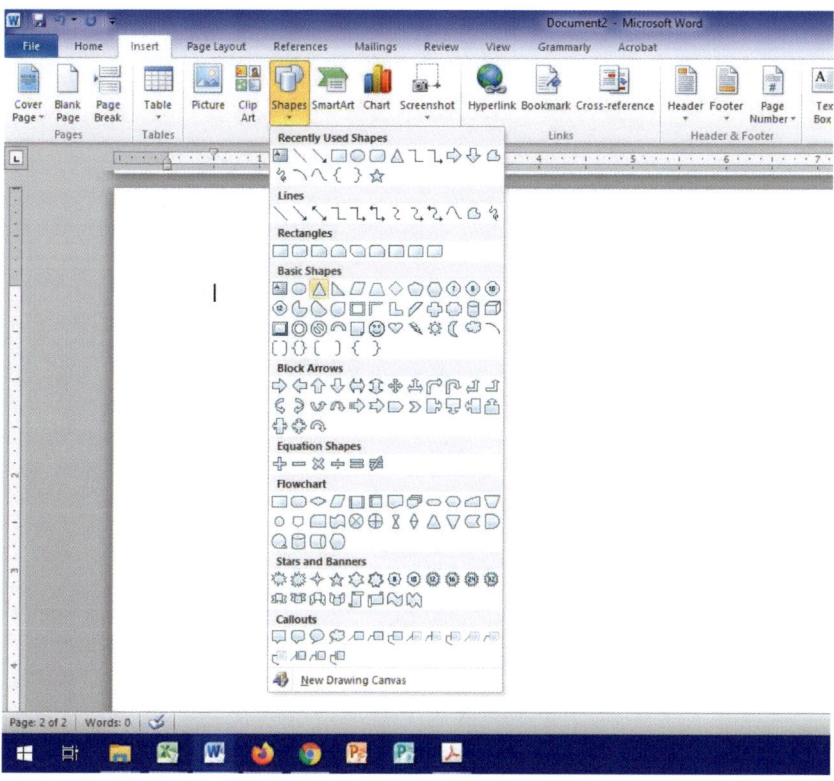

Place the triangle on the left side of the screen, and make the shape around the correct size. Right-click on the triangle with your mouse, then select the "Size and Position" header.

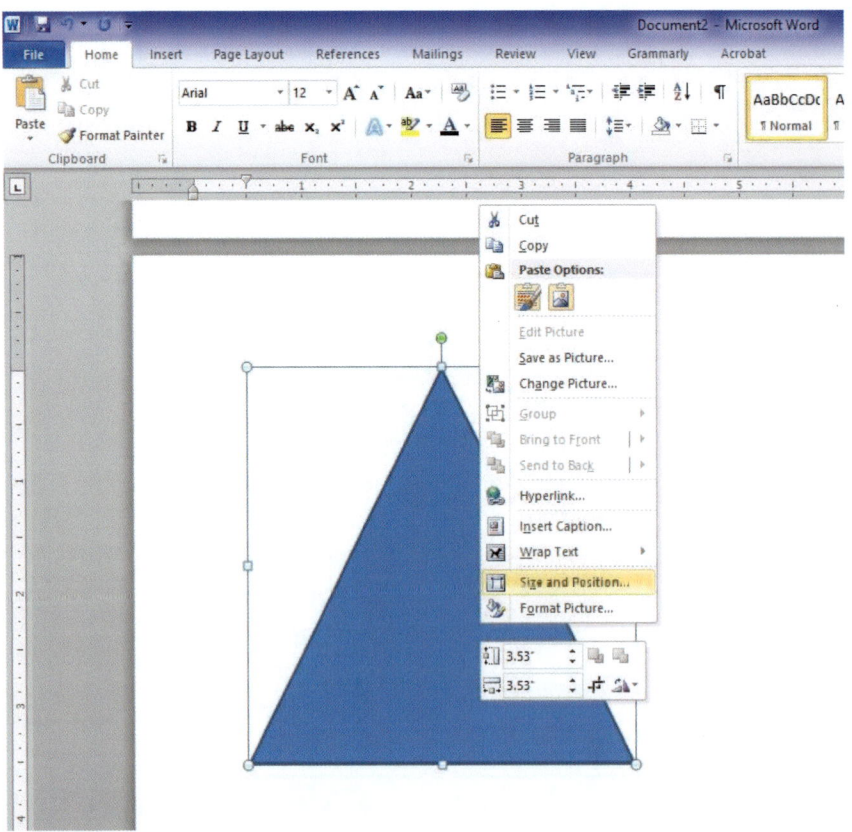

Click the tab labelled "Size", and made sure that the Height and Width of the shape are 3.5" (9cm). Please ensure that the box marked "Lock aspect ratio" is checked off. You have just made a perfect triangle. Next, you need to make another triangle to make the parallelogram.

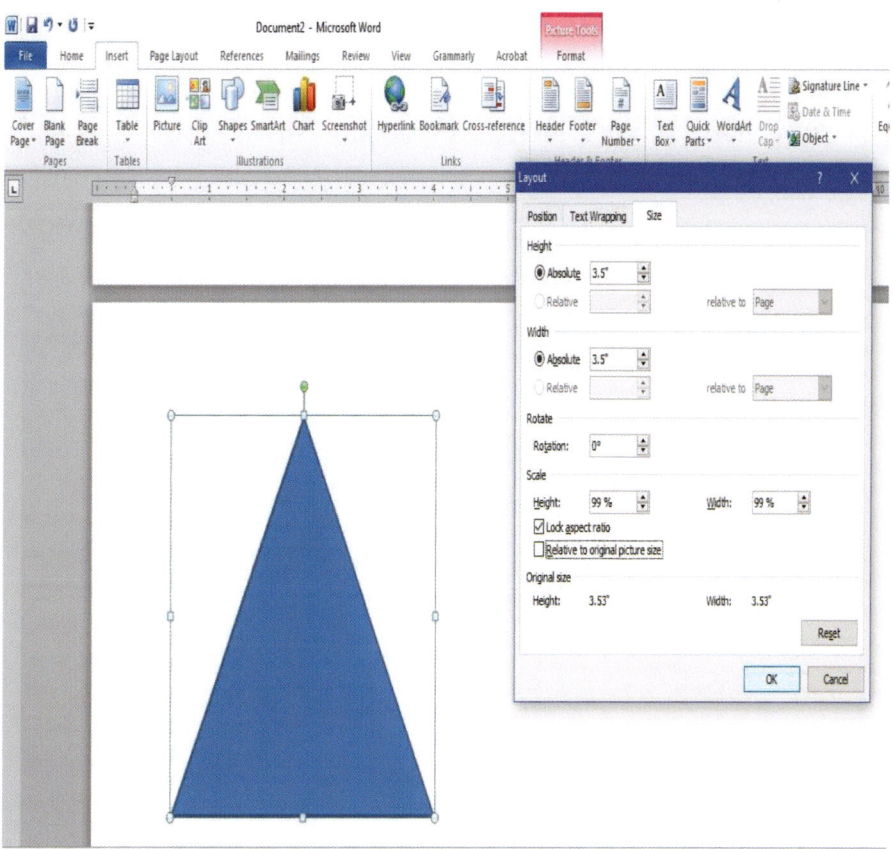

The next step is to copy and paste the triangle to make a second exact sized triangle. Once again you need to right-click your mouse. This time you will click on the "Format Picture" option. On the left hand side of the screen, you need to click on "3-D Rotation". Change the "Rotation" of "Axis Z" to 180° (Degrees).

Did I just give you an evil flashback to High School Geometry? Not to worry, the computer just did everything for you; fretting about proper angles is not allowed. Move your upside down triangle to the right side of the page. I use the ruler at the top of the page to eyeball a 3 ½" (9cm) distance between the two triangles. Adjust the margins if you need more room.

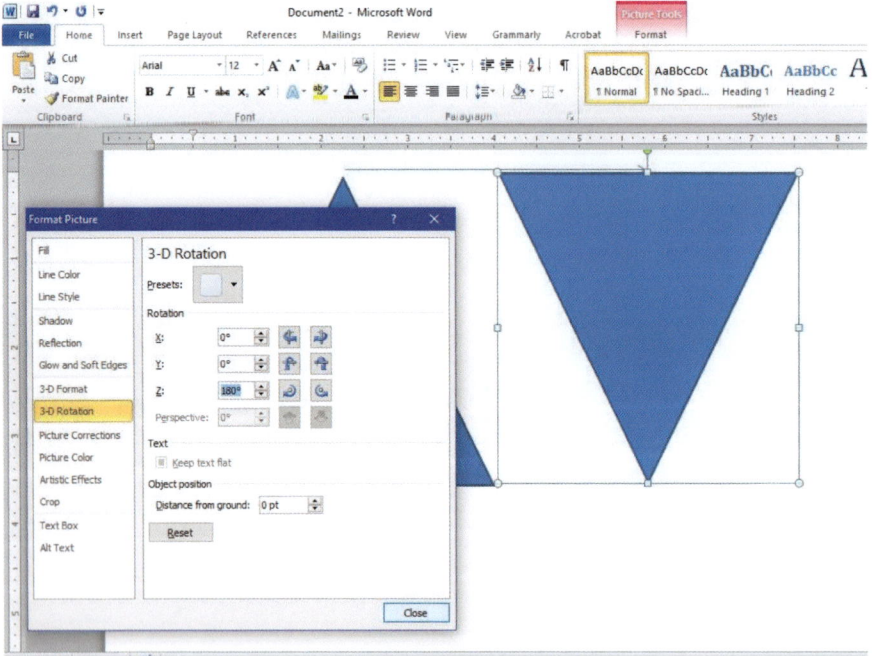

Going back to the "Insert" Tab, pull down the "Shapes" box again, but choose a straight line. Run a line between the top of the two triangles and the bottom of the triangles to form a parallelogram. (Is it just me or does the word parallelogram look like it's always spelled wrong?)

To ensure that you have created the proper distance, trust me and check, right-click each line and select size and position. The lines should be 3.5"(9cm) long. You might need to adjust the placement of the right triangle, but make sure the line is the proper length.

Once you have created this template you will need to print out two copies.

Carefully cut out the templates you have created. You will need two parallelograms for the red and green fabric. I have found that paper templates are too flimsy to hold up to the rigors of cutting fabric, so I reinforce the paper templates with sturdier material.

While a cardboard box is incredibly sturdy, I find that it is too thick for this application. Fabric tends to slip on me. Instead I use a file folder. Simply glue the templates to an old file folder, dry and then cut them out.

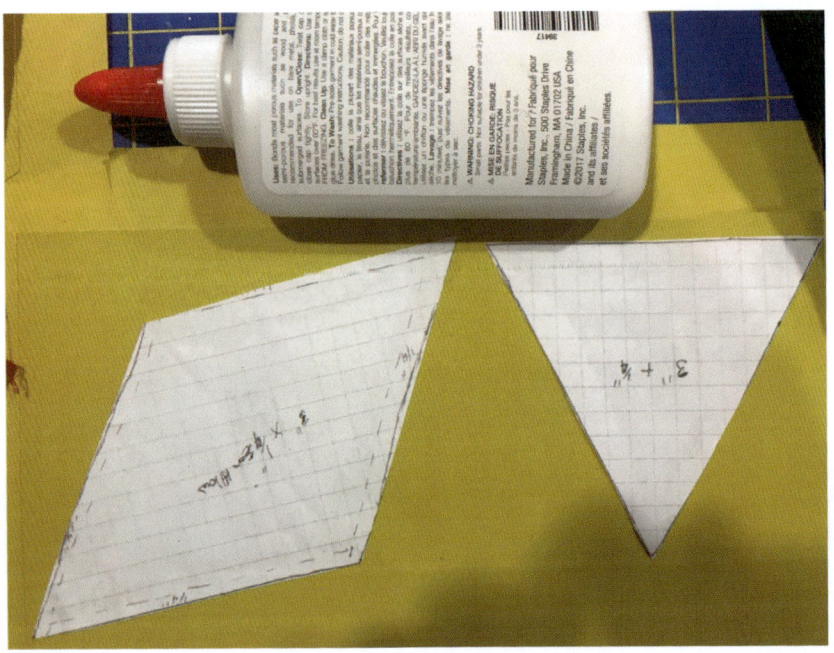

Begin Cutting Out Your Fabric

I mentioned using two parallelogram templates before. I generally flip one of the templates in the opposite direction, and label them. Using the design template, line up the parallelograms, and figure out which way the red and green fabric attaches to the triangle. From the template I made, the red fabric is the right sided parallelogram, and the green is the opposite direction.

Is this step absolutely necessary? Not in the least. The shapes you cut out are equidistant regardless of the orientation. Why do this step? It is great practice for when you want to create something in the same manner, but with different measurements.

On a self-healing cutting mat, place the fabric, the template, and sandwich them together using a ruler. Try to get the ruler to the edge of the template to ensure proper cutting. Can this step be done using scissors and traditional fabric pinning? Yes, but as much as I hate to admit it, using the mat and rotary cutter combination is faster and more accurate.

Cut out all the fabric before you begin sewing. I feel this is more efficient, and prevents any issues if you run out of a fabric before you have cut the amount you need. Using the design template, you will need to cut out the following: 15 red and 15 green parallelograms, 24 white fabric triangles, and 12 holly berry white triangles.

BEGIN PIECING TOGETHER YOUR QUILT

Now that you have all your pieces cut out, it is time to sew them together. Starting with Row 1, begin pinning and sewing each piece together. Follow the design template provided to place your pieces. I have added a quick graph if you are confused as to which way the pieces should be oriented.

Relax, it can always be fixed. You will probably make a mistake, and piece together a triangle and a red or green piece (I got tired of typing parallelogram…which I just did again! Sigh!) together incorrectly. Simply rip out the seam, and reorient, and resew.

ROW 1:

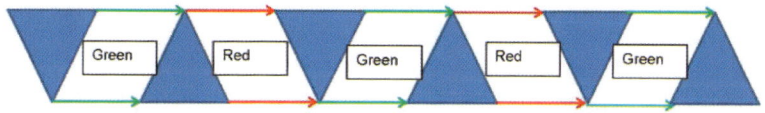

REMINDER: I designed this quilt to have a ¼" (1/2cm) seam allowance. Please remember to mark the seam or if your sewing machine has a guide utilize that feature.

Pressing your seams is an important part of any sewing project. In quilting, the standard is usually to press toward the darker color fabric. Tradition came from practicality. Hand sewing traditionally left gaps which could create the batting from oozing out of the quilt. Pressing the seam to one side, reinforced and covered the seams. The problem with pressing to one side is that it can cause humps to appear along the seams. Quilting by "Stitching in the Ditch" can alleviate this problem.

While I agree with this method to honor traditions, I *might* not have followed historical conventions. I had a little too much fun pressing open the seams, especially where the three fabrics met at the top of the triangle.

If you decide to be a rebel without a clue like me, beware of those judgmental people. They really like to scoff when you don't follow the rules. "It's my project, and I'll press like I want to…Nah-nah-nah-nah-na!"

While piecing together the fabric, you may run into a little bit of an overhang at the tips of the triangles. Simply snip the tips.

Sew Together the Rows

Once you have completed the first two rows, pin them together. This step is a great way to correct any sewing errors. Did you sew a 3/8" seam instead of a ¼"? This is not a problem. Put your fabric right sides together, and begin pinning in the following order.

Step One: Pin the tips of triangles together. Make sure they match.

Step Two: Pin the seams of the triangles that form diamonds together. Make sure the seams align together.

Step Three: Pin the center of each joined triangle. If there is an issue with a size difference, just create a little fold in the longer fabric when you pin the center. The entire 3D effect is dependent upon matching diamonds to form the block shape.

Step Four. Pin the center of each Quadrilateral (Also known as the parallelogram).

Step Five: Sew with a ¼" (1/2cm) seam.

After you have successfully sewn together the rows of fabric, press open the seams using an iron.

Prepare the Quilt for the Border

Now that the Tumbling Blocks have been assembled, it is time to create a border around the design. I chose solid green and red fabrics to highlight the interior of the Table Runner.

Before you begin measuring your border, first the top and bottom of the pattern need to be trimmed. Cut off the tops of the diamonds at the top and bottom of the quilt to make a straight line.

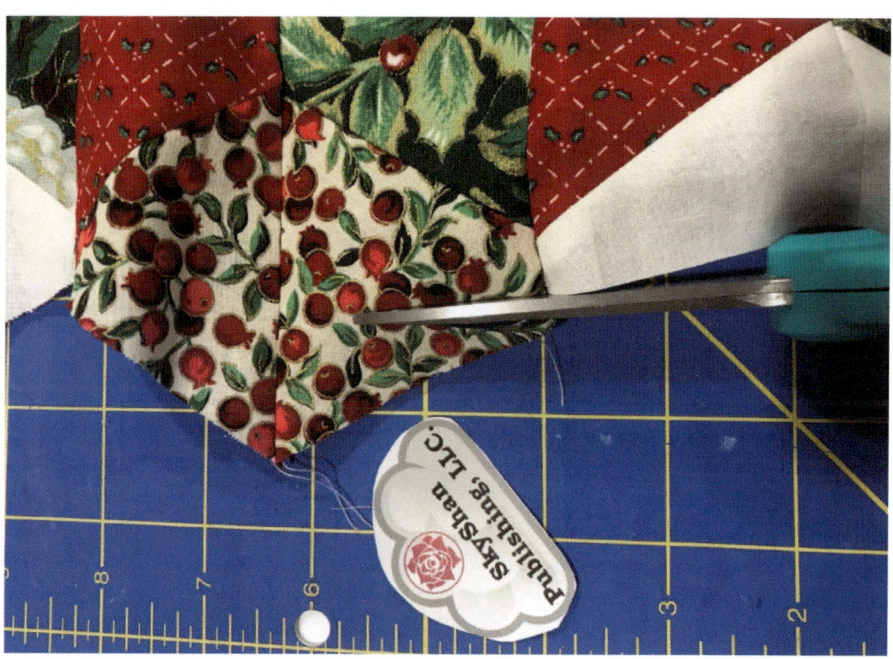

Create the Border to the Quilt

Measure and cut 2" (5cm) strips of fabric the length of the Tumbling Blocks plus ½" (1 1/4cm). I always cut the border slightly larger than the quilt to account for any errors in pinning and/or sewing. Pin the border to the Tumbling Blocks, right sides together, and sew with a ¼" (0.5cm) seam allowance.

Press the seam, and trim any excess fabric from the border.

To create the red triangles at either end of the Table Runner, fold the fabric in half, and press with an iron. Measure the length of the Tumbling Blocks interior, excluding the green border; this will be the bottom of the quilt's width. Next, measure about two thirds the length of the width for the length of your Triangle. For example, I made a triangle with the dimensions 13 ½"(34 1/4 cm) x 9 ½" (24 1/4 cm) x 9 ½". Unfold the fabric, and cut to make two triangles from the square of fabric.

Sew the red triangle to the Tumbling Blocks portion of the table runner. Center this piece as best as you can.

Cut 4 (four) additional 2" (5cm) strips of green fabric. Make sure these strips are at least 4-5" (10-12cm) longer than you need. Pin the first green strip, making sure the strip extends at least an inch past the top and the bottom green strip. Take the second strip, and pin right sides together. You are going to cross the strip at the top that has already been sewn into place. This will create the top of the triangle.

At the bottom of the triangle, sew the strip to the border edge of the green. TIP: Line up your sewing machine with the seam line of the red fabric. Use this line to extend the seam onto the green border. This will give you the correct allowance, and look of the seam. Trim the excess green fabric.

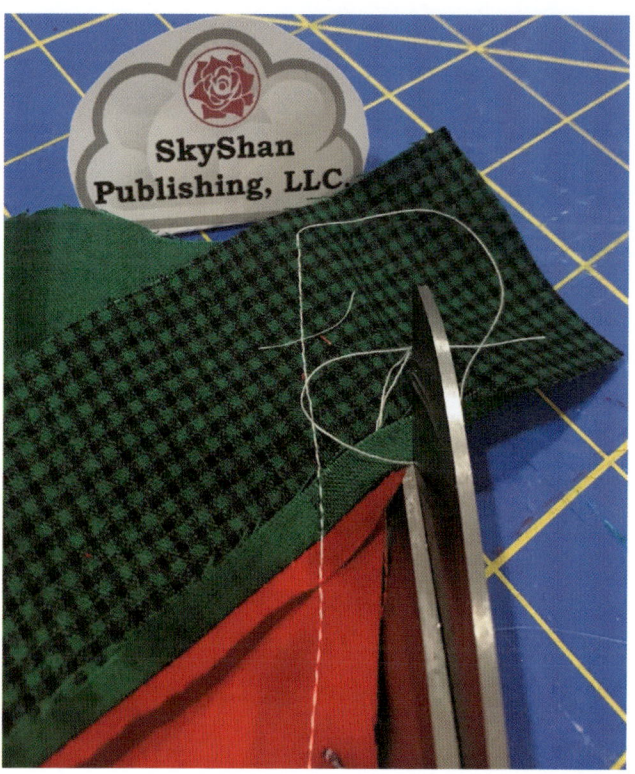

The top of your table runner is done. The next step is to prepare the top for quilting.

Prepare the Table Runner for Quilting

Fold over ¼" (1/2cm) of material on the top of the table runner and press. This will be the method to bind the quilt. Stich this closed using a similar colored thread.

The next step is to choose and cut the batting. The most common batting choices are polyester and cotton. Through trial and error, I prefer using cotton. My preference has nothing to do with workability and everything to do with how the polyester feels when I touch it. It gives me the heebie-jeebies, and you can't fall into a Zen crafting headspace while feeling phantom ants crawling over your skin.

Some people also choose to use a more economical option. My opinions are my own, but I will give you my two cents on my experiences. Felt is very economical, but my sewing machine had a very difficult time quilting, even with a walking foot. Using excess fabric is gaining in popularity amongst the frugal set, but if it is not very light the color can bleed through. Furthermore, I feel (Opinion only feel free to disagree) that the quilt is not thick enough to give the quilting enough depth.

As this quilt is a non-standard shape, lay the top of the table runner over your batting. Secure the top to the batting with safety pins or straight pins. Cut out the batting, trimming the batting to be slightly smaller than the quilt top.

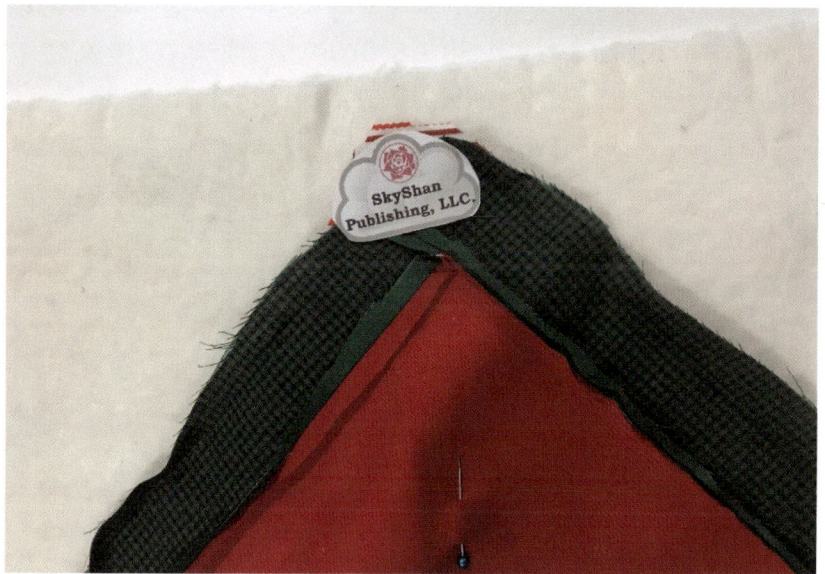

Take the fabric you chose for the back of the Table Runner Quilt, and lay the table runner top over of the backing. Safety pin the top to the bottom of the fabric to prevent slippage. Cut the fabric for the bottom of the quilt about ½" (1 1/4cm) wider than the quilt topper.

Sandwich the batting between the Quilt Topper and the bottom. Ensure right sides are outside. Safety pin all three layers together. Start from the middle, and work your way out towards the sides. Run your hands gently over the top of the quilt as you pin, working your way out from the center as you pin.

Quilt the Table Runner

If you are using your sewing machine to quilt this project, I strongly recommend using a walking foot. This is a situation of being "Penny wise and pound foolish". Spend the extra money to make yourself successful. Without a walking foot, disaster can strike.

If you decide to hand quilt this project, I suggest using an embroidery hoop. This will keep the fabrics and batting stable, and prevent the fabric from slipping.

I recommend quilting "In the Ditch". This term is used to describe both quilting directly in the seams, and running stiches to one side of the seams. I use this term to describe quilting slightly off center. I want my work to be seen, and I think it looks better.

I outlined the Tumbling Blocks in this quilt. I used white thread to help the quilting pop.

Finish Binding your Quilt

The excess fabric on the bottom of the table runner will be folded over, and pinned to the green fabric border.

Pin the two sides together, ensuring that the bottom fabric is slightly under the green edge.

When you get to the corners, fold over the fabric in the direction you are going in. The overhanging fabric in the other direction is then folded over in the opposite direction. Ensure the folds remain hidden under the quilt.

You've Reached the Finish Line

Congratulations! You've made it to the end. If you have followed along, you should be ready to entertain for the holidays in stylish fashion.

I hope you have enjoyed this guide. I have a few other frugal crafting books that I have been creating. I hope you will give them a try.

ALSO AVAILABLE FROM SKYSHAN PUBLISHING –

ABOUT THE AUTHOR

Andrea Reynolds has always had an incredible imagination. She is the international bestselling author of over twenty books. Her love of crafting has brought her more joy and peace than any other activity. She just wishes she could draw a stick figure. She is the mother of two beautiful children, and one rescue dog. When not writing, her head will be found stuck in her crafting closet.